Mapping Britain's Landscapes

Cities, Towns and Villages

Jen Green

FRANKLIN WATTS
LONDON•SYDNEY

First published in 2007 by Franklin Watts

Copyright © Franklin Watts 2007

Franklin Watts
338 Euston Road
London NW1 3BH

Franklin Watts Australia
Level 17/207 Kent Street
Sydney, NSW 2000

Series editor: Sarah Peutrill
Art director: Jonathan Hair
Design: White Design
Additional map illustrations: John Alston
Consultant: Steve Watts

A CIP catalogue record for this book is available
from the British Library.

Dewey number: 526.09141
ISBN: 978 0 7496 7114 3

Printed in China

Franklin Watts is a division of Hachette Children's
Books, an Hachette Livre UK company.

Picture credits:
Chris Andrews/Corbis: 1,19. Graham Bell/PD:13.
Jason Hawkes/Corbis: front cover r, 23. Jason
Hawkes/Image Bank/Getty Images: 27. Ordnance
Survey © Crown copyright 2007: front cover l.
Ordnance Survey © Crown copyright 2007
supplied by mapsinternational.co.uk: 9, 10, 14,
17, 21, 22, 24, 28, 29. Reuters/Corbis: 25. G R
Richardson/Superstock: 7. Simmons
Aerofilms/Getty Images: 15. Sandy
Stockwell/LAP/Corbis: 11, 16, 20. Stone/Getty
Images: 5. Woodmansterne/Topfoto: 8, 18. Every
attempt has been made to clear copyright. Should
there be any inadvertent omission please apply to
the publisher for rectification.

Note to parents and teachers: Every effort has
been made by the Publishers to ensure that the
websites in this book are suitable for children,
that they are of the highest educational value,
and that they contain no inappropriate or
offensive material. However, because of the
nature of the Internet, it is impossible to
guarantee that the contents of these sites will not
be altered. We strongly advise that Internet access
is supervised by a responsible adult.

Contents

What are cities, towns and villages?

Cities, towns and villages are all settlements – places where people live. Settlements are shown on maps, along with features such as roads. Learning to read maps can help you to explore settlements.

FROM SMALL BEGINNINGS

Settlements come in many shapes and sizes. The smallest settlements, farms and hamlets, hold less than 50 people. Villages contain a few hundred people. Towns contain anything from 1,000 to 100,000 people. Settlements larger than that are called cities.

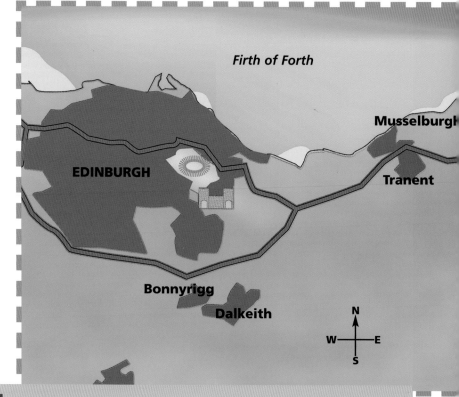

Firth of Forth

Musselburgh

EDINBURGH

Tranent

Bonnyrigg

Dalkeith

N
W   E
S

Map Key

Settlement

Major road

Sea

Beach

Castle

Arthur's Seat

↓ Using the map

What are maps?
Maps are drawings of the landscape from above. Maps show areas of different sizes, from local maps to maps of the whole country. The larger the area shown, the less detail is included. Maps that show a large area help you find your way.

Maps use symbols – pictures, lines, colours or letters – to show what's on the ground. Symbols make the map less crowded, so it is easier to read. The map key explains what the symbols mean. Find the map key features (left) on the map.

↑ **This photo shows the city of Edinburgh in Scotland, and the surrounding countryside.**

Look at the photo and the map

→ A hill called Arthur's Seat is one of the main features in the photo. You can also see a castle. Find these on the map.

→ Maps only show permanent features such as roads and built-up areas. Photos may show temporary features such as the weather, cars and people. What temporary features can you see in the photo?

URBAN AND RURAL AREAS

A few hundred years ago, most people in Britain lived in rural areas – the countryside. Now 85 percent of people live in urban areas – towns and cities. But small settlements still far outnumber large ones. Britain has over 40,000 villages and 12,800 towns, but only 60 cities. People live in different ways in urban and rural areas.

TAKING IT FURTHER

What size of settlement do you live in – is it a village, a town or a city? Look at the area where you live on a road atlas. What is the largest settlement in the area?

Where do settlements grow up?

Settlements are collections of houses along with the services that local people need – anything from post boxes to shops, schools and sports centres. But why do settlements grow up in a particular location, and not somewhere else?

BY FOOD AND WATER

In Britain, many settlements are hundreds of years old. In early times, the most important needs were food and water. Villages grew up near streams and rivers that provided fresh water. There was often fertile land nearby, where crops could be grown. Local forests yielded wood for building and fuel.

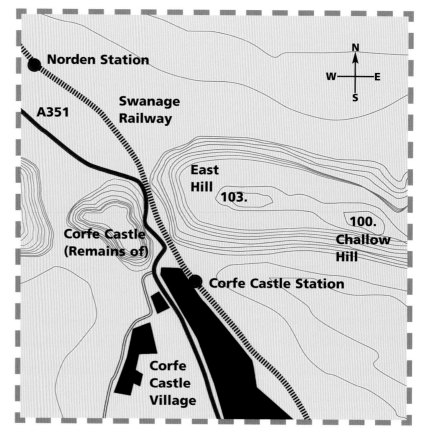

Map Key

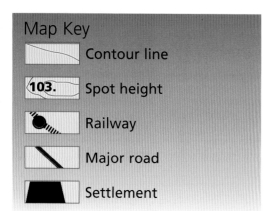

Contour line

103. Spot height

Railway

Major road

Settlement

⬇ Using the map

Contour lines
Hills, valleys and slopes are shown on maps using contour lines. These brown lines join places at the same height above sea level. When the slope is steep the contour lines are drawn close together. The height of particular places is shown by numbers called spot heights. Local services are also shown. Find the map key features.

↑ **The photo shows the village of Corfe Castle and the remains of its hilltop fort.**

Look at the photo and the map

→ The photo shows a ridge of high ground, called East Hill, behind the fort. Find it on the map. What is the height of the ridge?

→ The photo shows steep slopes on both the fort mound and also East Hill. How are steep slopes shown on the map?

→ The map shows a deep valley between the fort and East Hill. Look on the map to see what the valley is used for.

HILLTOP SETTLEMENTS

Many early settlements grew up near hills, which were used as lookouts. From the hill, people could see an enemy approaching. Settlements grew up around these forts. A hilltop fort provided safety in time of war. Crops grew well in nearby lowlands. Corfe Castle in southern Britain is a village with a hilltop fort.

TAKING IT FURTHER

• How old is the city, town or village where you live? Use your local library or the Internet to find out when it was founded – the date the first buildings appeared.
• Study a map of your local area. Are there any hills nearby? Look for spot heights to find out the height of local high points. Now check the contour lines on the map. Are the slopes steep or gradual?

Settlements by rivers

Many settlements in Britain have grown up by rivers. In ancient times, rivers had many uses, besides providing drinking water. Rivers continue to be useful today, but sometimes for different reasons.

EARLY RIVER SETTLEMENTS

From early times, river valleys provided fertile land where crops grew well. Valleys also created useful routes through hills and mountains. Settlements grew up where rivers could be crossed by bridges, or in shallow places where they could be forded. Towns with names such as Oxford and Cambridge began in this way.

Look at the photo and the map

→ The photo shows a cathedral and several bridges. Find these features on the map.

→ What are the advantages of Durham's position? Can you see any disadvantages?

→ Lay a piece of thin string along the curves of the river. Measure the string along the scale bar to find out the length of the river's loop.

TRANSPORT AND ENERGY

Rivers themselves are also used for travel. Goods and people can be transported for many kilometres along these watery highways. The force of swift-running rivers can be used to work machinery in factories and mills.

← The photo shows the old centre of Durham surrounded by a loop of the river. The city is located on a hill, safe from floods.

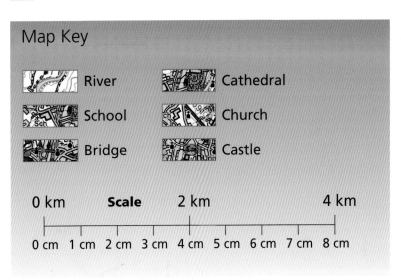

DEFENCE

Rivers are also useful for defence. The city of Durham in northeastern England grew up on a great loop of the River Wear, called a meander. The city was very difficult to attack because it is almost entirely surrounded by water.

TAKING IT FURTHER

Find Durham and the River Wear on a UK atlas or road map. Use string to trace the course of the river from the source (start) to the sea. Lay the string along the map scale to work out the river's length.

↓ Using the map

OS maps
This map was made by Britain's official map-making organisation, Ordnance Survey (OS). OS maps show public buildings and services such as schools, hospitals and churches and a lot more. The scale bar at the bottom allows you to estimate distances on the map.

Map Key

River   Cathedral

School   Church

Bridge   Castle

0 km	Scale	2 km		4 km

0 cm   1 cm   2 cm   3 cm   4 cm   5 cm   6 cm   7 cm   8 cm

Settlements by the sea

Cities, towns and villages can be found all around Britain's coastline. Coastal settlements can grow and thrive, or shrink, for different reasons. These reasons can also change over the years.

IN THE PAST

In ancient times, people settled on coasts because the sea provided food. Many coastal towns began as tiny fishing villages. The sea also provided transport, both around Britain's coast and across to Europe. Ports grew up on bays and inlets that made good harbours for ships.

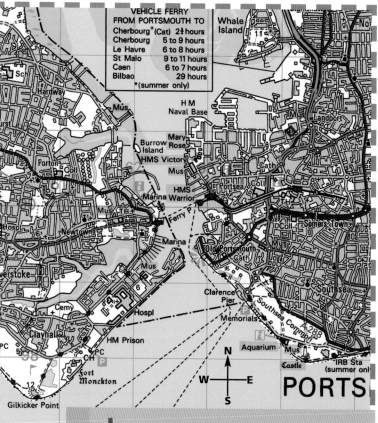

VEHICLE FERRY FROM PORTSMOUTH TO	
Cherbourg*(Cat)	2¾ hours
Cherbourg	5 to 9 hours
Le Havre	6 to 8 hours
St Malo	9 to 11 hours
Caen	6 to 7 hours
Bilbao	29 hours
*(summer only)	

↓ Using the map

Points of the compass
The points of the compass: north, south, east and west, can help you find your way on maps, and also on the ground. North is at the top on most maps. You can locate places on the map by giving their direction from somewhere else. For example, the aquarium in the bottom right-hand corner lies east of the prison at bottom left.

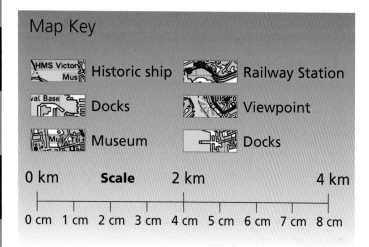

Map Key

	Historic ship		Railway Station
	Docks		Viewpoint
	Museum		Docks

0 km	**Scale**	2 km	4 km

0 cm   1 cm   2 cm   3 cm   4 cm   5 cm   6 cm   7 cm   8 cm

Ports such as Portsmouth, Bristol, Liverpool and Glasgow became major centres for industry and shipbuilding. Local factories used raw materials that arrived by sea. The docks were also used to send finished goods abroad.

→ **The photo shows the naval docks at Portsmouth. This area is shown at the top of the map. You can tell by comparing the shapes of the docks in the photo and on the map.**

Look at the photo and the map

→ **The photo shows several ships and the railway station. Which of these features can you find on the map?**

→ **The map shows the location of the original port – Old Portsmouth. Why do you think a port grew up here?**

→ **Portsmouth is popular with tourists, as well as being a busy port and naval centre. Look at the map and list five things for tourists to do here.**

TOURISM

In the last century or so, tourism has become a major industry in many coastal settlements. People come to swim, use the beach or go boating or wind-surfing.

TAKING IT FURTHER

• Look on a UK atlas to locate the coastline nearest you. What ports and other settlements can you find there?

• Study the shape of the coastline to work out the advantages of these locations. Are settlements located on beaches, natural harbours or a river mouth?

• Use the Internet or your local library to find out the main industry in the nearest coastal town. Find out whether this work is the same as it was 100 years ago.

Mining and industry

Some settlements in Britain have grown up near sources of raw materials including minerals such as iron, tin and coal.

COAL MINING

Coal mining became important in the early 1800s. At this time, called the Industrial Revolution, machines were invented to do all kinds of work. Factories were built in many parts of Britain, and coal was needed to run the machinery.

COAL AND SOUTH WALES

Before 1800, the valleys of South Wales were remote, with small farming villages. Then coal was discovered here, and many mines opened. Ironworks were built to produce iron using local iron ore and coal. Villages such as Rhondda (see photograph), grew rapidly during the 1800s as people came to work in the mines. Roads and railways were built to carry coal and iron to cities and ports.

↓ Using the map

Land use maps
Land use maps, like this one, show the natural resources of an area. This map shows the location of coal and iron ore in South Wales. It also shows the location of ironworks, where iron ore was smelted, or heated, to make iron.

Map Key

☐	Coalfield	⬛	Main town
●▶●	Ironworks in 1800		
⬛	Rocks containing iron ore		
⬛○	Coalmine in 1997		

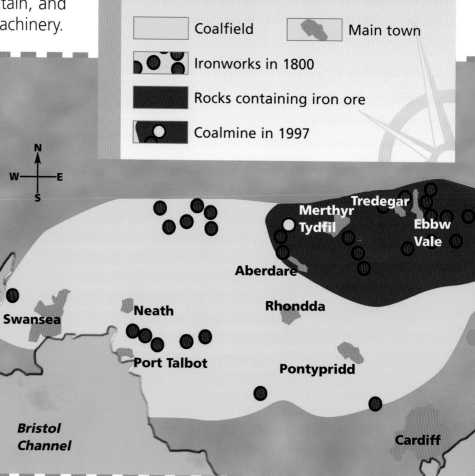

N
W ← → E
S

Tredegar
Merthyr
Tydfil
Ebbw
Vale
Aberdare
Rhondda
Neath
Swansea
Port Talbot
Pontypridd
Bristol
Channel
Cardiff

↑ **The mining village of Rhondda in South Wales.**

SHRINKING SETTLEMENTS

Settlements can start to shrink if the work that brought people to the area is no longer available. From the 1920s, Welsh mining villages started to shrink when mines and factories started to close because the local coal and iron was used up.

TAKING IT FURTHER

• Look up the Rhondda Valley on a UK atlas. A good transport network is vital to all industrial areas. List all the forms of transport you can see in the region today.
• Find out about the types of work that go on in your area. Are there any factories, and if so, what do they produce?

Look at the photo and the map

→ The map shows the location of ironworks in South Wales around 1800. Can you explain why ironworks were built in these locations?

→ In 1800, less than 550 people lived in the Rhondda Valley. By 1925, 170,000 people were living in Rhondda. However by 1990, there were only 80,000 people. Can you explain why?

→ This photo was taken looking up the Rhondda Valley from above Pontypridd. Look at the photo and map. In which direction was the photographer facing?

Village life

Only 15 percent of people in Britain live in rural areas. Small settlements such as villages are peaceful, and usually less polluted than towns and cities. However there are also drawbacks, including fewer jobs.

↓ Using the map

Grid references

On OS maps, blue lines form a grid of squares. On this map, the lines running up are marked with letters. The lines running across are numbered. The letters and numbers form a grid reference that helps you locate places on the map. The reference gives the bottom left corner of the square. For example, South Zeal is in square C3.

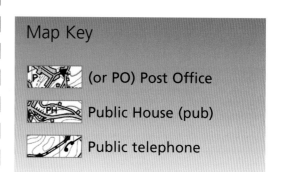

Map Key

P	(or PO) Post Office
PH	Public House (pub)
	Public telephone

VILLAGE SERVICES

The smaller the settlement, the fewer services it has. Small villages such as South Zeal in Devon, shown here, may have a post box, public telephone, bus stop and village hall. There may also be a church, pub and a primary school. Larger villages and small towns have many more services, including shops, restaurants, a library, doctor's surgery and secondary school.

Look at the photo and the map

→ Settlements have different shapes, which can provide clues as to how they grew up. Settlements that grow up along roads are long and thin. This is called a linear settlement. Find a settlement like this on the map.

→ Other settlements have a compact, rounded shape. They are called nucleated settlements because they grew up around a centre or nucleus. Find a settlement like this on the map.

→ Study the map. List all the services you can see in the villages of Sticklepath, South Tawton and South Zeal. Which village has the most services?

→ The grid squares on a map can also be used to estimate distance. Each side of the square represents 1 km. Use the grid to estimate the distance between Sticklepath in B4 and West Wyke in C2.

CHANGING LIFE

Twenty years ago, most villages had a shop. Now many local shops have closed, and people shop at supermarkets instead. Jobs are also scarce in rural areas. Many people travel to the nearest town or city to work, by train, bus or car. This is called commuting, and the regions around cities where commuters live are called commuter belts.

TAKING IT FURTHER

Look at the villages in your area on a local map or road atlas. Study the shapes of villages. What types of settlement are they? What services can you see marked on the map?

↑ **The village of South Zeal in Devon.**

Urban life

Most people in Britain live in large towns and cities. Large settlements have more services and better transport. There are also many more jobs. People living in the city and surrounding settlements find work in factories, offices and running local services.

→ The photo shows the centre of Cardiff with the Millennium Stadium. Find it on the map.

Look at the photo and the map

→ Cardiff was once the main port for the South Wales coalfields (see pages 12/13). Now tourism is more important. Look at the map and photo, and list all the features you can see that attract visitors to Cardiff.

→ The map also shows Cardiff's educational and administrative buildings. Which can you find?

URBAN SERVICES

The larger the settlement, the more services it has. Large towns have many shops, restaurants and places of worship. There will be a choice of schools and doctors' surgeries, along with colleges and hospitals. There are recreation centres such as cinemas, theatres and sports centres.

Cities have even more services, such as universities, museums, sports stadiums and art galleries. Britain's capital cities, London, Edinburgh and Cardiff, have government buildings too.

↓ Using a map

Grid numbers

On OS maps all the grid lines are numbered. The grid reference gives the east-west distance on the lines running upwards first, followed by the north-south distance on the lines running across. Remember this order with the phrase "Along the corridor and up the stairs". For example, City Hall is in square 1876. Write down all the features you can see in 1876. What is the grid reference for the Central Station?

TAKING IT FURTHER

• Use the Internet or local library to find out how many people live in your town, or the nearest large settlement. This is called the town's population.

• Study your town on a local map. List all the services such as schools, colleges and sports centres, that you can see.

CITY DISTRICTS

In big cities, buildings with the same function are often grouped into districts. For example, there are residential districts where people live, shopping centres, and industrial districts with factories. Most offices are in the commercial district. The administrative district holds council offices.

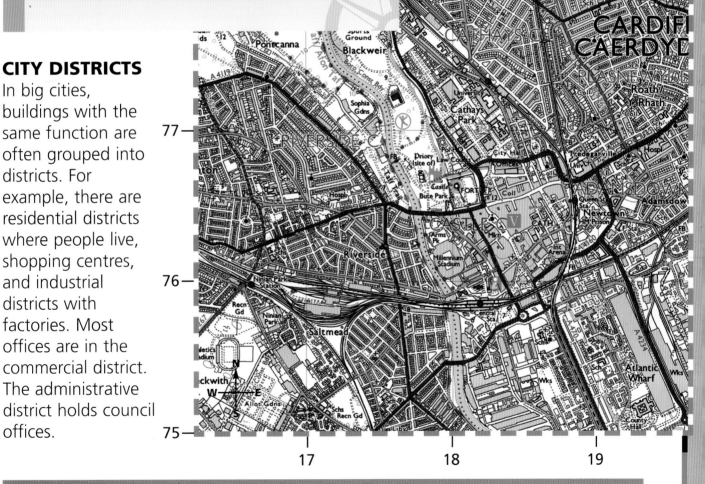

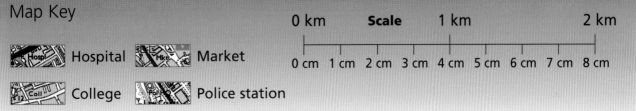

Map Key

Hospital   Market

College   Police station

How do settlements grow and change?

Settlements never stay exactly the same. Small changes are always happening, as people add a room to their house, or a new shop opens. Sometimes major changes happen quickly, for example when a new housing estate or motorway is built. The work that goes on also changes over the years.

↓ Using the map

Old maps

This map shows the city of Bath in 1786. It has no grid, but the style of showing rivers, roads and public buildings is similar to that on modern maps. North is at the top, as on modern maps. Modern maps are drawn with the help of aerial photos taken by aircraft and satellites. But this map was made without the use of photos.

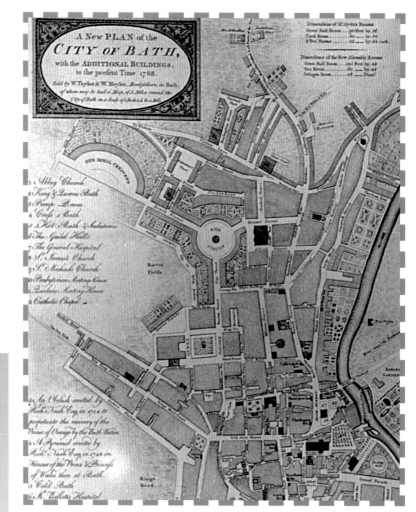

BATH

Bath, in southwest England, is one of Britain's oldest cities. The Romans founded a city here in 44 CE, at the site of some warm mineral springs. During the 1700s, Bath became a fashionable health resort. The city grew quickly at this time, and streets of fine houses were built. Later Bath became a manufacturing centre, but now tourism is the main industry.

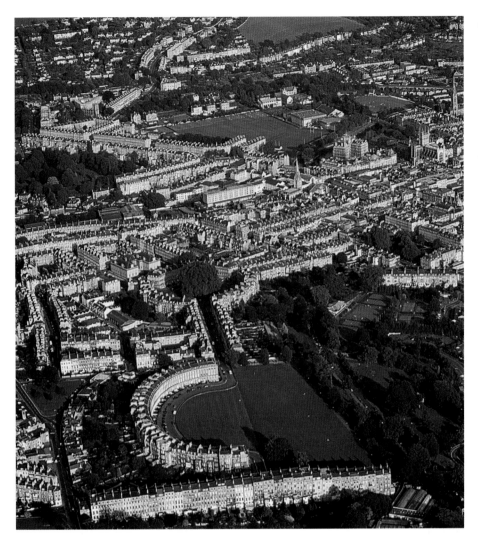

• Road atlases have detailed maps of city centres. Find a road atlas map of Bath. Compare the layout of the town today with the 1786 map. How has the city changed?

• Think about how the settlement where you live has changed in the last few years. Have new roads or housing estates been built? Now try to find out how the settlement has changed in the last 50 or 100 years. You may be able to find an old map. Or you could ask older people about what the area was like when they first lived there.

↑ **The photo shows two of Bath's most famous landmarks: the curving lines of the Royal Crescent and the Circus. Both areas were built in the 1700s.**

NEW DEVELOPMENTS

Most towns and cities in Britain have grown and changed a lot since the 1700s. Bath has changed less than most. Every city, town and village has a local council, which checks all new developments. Bath has strict rules for building, so the historic centre, which attracts tourists, is not spoiled.

Look at the photo and the map

→ **Find the Royal Crescent and the Circus in the northwest of the city on the map.**

→ **The photo was taken from a plane. Look at the photo and map to work out in which direction the photograph was taken. The distinctive layout of the streets provides a clue.**

→ **Can you explain why a city grew up in this location? How has the work that goes on in Bath changed over the years?**

Britain's capital

London is Britain's capital and largest city. Almost 2,000 years ago, the Romans built a fortified city called Londinium at a good crossing point on the River Thames. Sea-going ships could sail upriver as far as London, linking it with Europe and beyond. The city became a major trading centre. In the 1700s and 1800s it was the capital of a huge empire.

Look at the photo and the map

→ The photo shows many high-rise buildings. Are these shown on the map?

→ The photo shows two bridges beyond the Millennium Wheel (London Eye). The map shows one is a road bridge, but what is the purpose of the other, Hungerford Bridge?

→ Parks and open spaces are important in cities. Name a park or garden shown on the map.

BIG BUSINESSES

London is still a leading centre for business, banking and trade. Tourism is also now a major industry in London. Visitors come to see landmarks such as St Paul's Cathedral and the Tower of London, and explore London's world-class museums, theatres and art galleries.

← The photo shows some of the most famous sights of London, including the Houses of Parliament and the Millennium Wheel or 'London Eye' across the river. Can you see them on the map?

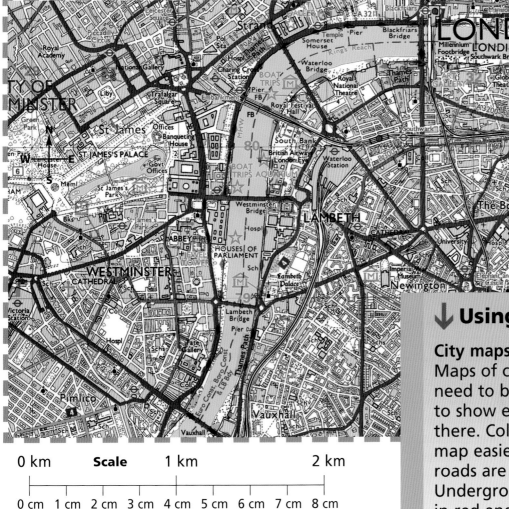

```
0 km          Scale          1 km                              2 km
├─────────────────────────────┼──────────────────────────────────┤
0 cm  1 cm  2 cm  3 cm  4 cm  5 cm  6 cm  7 cm  8 cm
```

CITY ZONES

Like other cities, London contains several zones, arranged in rings about the centre. On a journey into London, you pass through the outer suburbs with large houses and new estates, to the inner suburbs with terraced houses and apartment blocks. You then reach a zone that was once industrial, but now has many flats and offices, to arrive in the centre, with many high-rise buildings.

TAKING IT FURTHER

- Look at an atlas map showing the whole of London, with the River Thames snaking through it. Why do you think the capital grew up here?
- What are the advantages of living in such a large city? What are the disadvantages?

↓ Using the map

City maps

Maps of central London need to be very detailed, to show everything that is there. Colours make the map easier to read. Major roads are red or orange. Underground stations are in red and are easy to pick out. Places of interest for tourists have blue symbols.

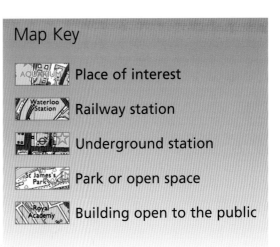

Map Key

AQUARIUM	Place of interest
Waterloo Station	Railway station
⊕	Underground station
St James's Park	Park or open space
Royal Academy	Building open to the public

New developments

Most settlements grow slowly and steadily. Some start from scratch and grow in just a few years. New developments are carefully planned to meet the needs of local people.

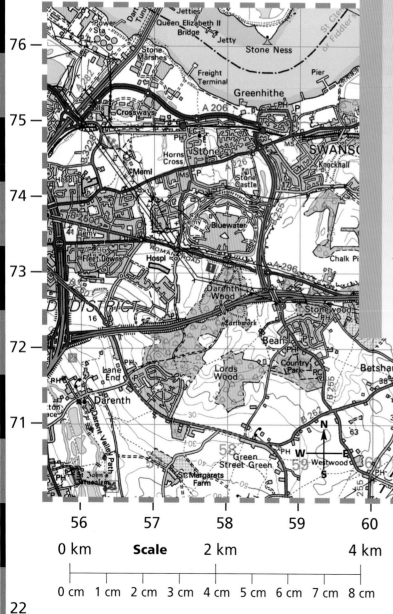

↓ Using the map

Scale on maps

All maps show the landscape reduced to a particular size, or scale. On this 1:50,000 map, every 1 cm on the map represents 500 m (0.5 km) on the ground. On 1:25,000 maps (such as on page 17) 1 cm represents 250 m. The area shown is smaller and the map is more detailed. The scale bar shows the scale. The squares on a map can also be used to estimate the time journeys will take. If you walk at 4 km/hr, you cover four squares in an hour on the map (left), or one square every 15 minutes. Look at the map and guess how long it would take to walk from Stone railway station in square 5774 to the hospital in 5773.

NEW TOWNS

Between the 1940s and 1970s, over 20 new towns were built in Britain. Milton Keynes, Corby, Telford and other new towns were designed with wide streets and large gardens. These settlements were planned to reduce overcrowding in cities.

Look at the photo and the map

→ A good transport network is vital to out-of-town shopping centres. What transport links can you see in the photo and on the map?

→ Look up Bluewater on a UK atlas. Why was this a good site for a shopping centre?

GREEN BELTS

At the same time, planners established a ring of open countryside around London and other cities, where no one could build without special permission. These areas, designed to prevent cities spreading, are called green belts.

SHOPPING CENTRES

Since the 1970s no more new towns have been built, but out-of-town shopping centres have sprung up. These usually lie close to several towns and have good transport networks. Superstores, shops, cafés and restaurants are all close together. These developments are often built on cheap land which was once waste ground or a factory.

↑ This photo shows Bluewater Shopping Centre near Dartford, east of London. It has been designed around several lakes, hence the name.

TAKING IT FURTHER

Try planning your own new town! All towns need places for people to live, work and go to school. People also need services such as hospitals and libraries, and places for recreation such as parks, sports centres and swimming pools. Try making a map of your ideal town.

Getting about

An effective transport network is vital to all cities, towns and villages. Yet transport can cause problems. In small settlements there is often too little public transport. People have to rely on cars to get about.

↓ Using the map

Transport maps
This map of central Glasgow shows the transport network, including railway and underground stations, roads, parking and a pedestrian area where cars are not allowed. The streets are named. Major roads keep cars out of the centre.

- Compare the transport map with OS maps shown in this book. What differences do you notice?
- Study the map and list all the forms of transport that you could use to get about in Glasgow. Where would you expect not to see cars?
- Use the map scale to estimate the distance from High Street station in the east to the main Queen Street station.

RUSH HOUR
As Britain's towns and cities grew up quickly, it has been difficult for transport services to keep pace. Trains and buses are now often overcrowded during rush hours, when people travel to and from work. In urban areas there are just too many cars on the road. This leads to traffic jams and parking problems. Vehicles also give off exhaust fumes which pollute the air.

↑ Traffic is often heavy on city roads.

SOLVING TRAFFIC PROBLEMS
Local councils can reduce traffic problems by improving public transport. Ring roads and bypasses carry traffic away from city centres. However these new roads can harm the countryside. Many towns have park-and-ride schemes. People leave their cars on the outskirts and travel into town by bus. Cleaner forms of transport, such as electric trams, reduce pollution. Special lanes can make journeys quicker for bus users and cyclists.

TAKING IT FURTHER
- List all the forms of transport used in the settlement where you live. Is it easy to get about? Try to find out how your local council is tackling transport problems. Are there bus and cycle lanes, and a park-and-ride scheme?
- What actions can councils take to reduce traffic jams in city centres?

Looking to the future

Cities and large towns have more jobs and services than small settlements. However, cities can also have problems. They can be overcrowded. They can also damage the environment, for example by producing huge amounts of waste. They also use a lot of energy.

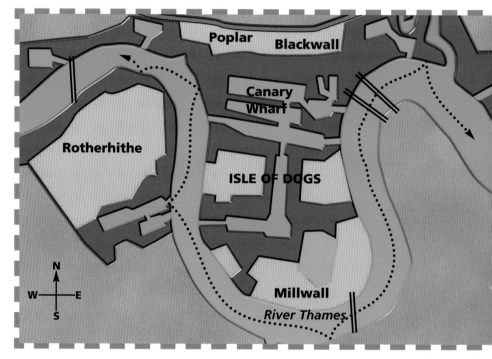

↓ Using the map

Land use maps
This map shows London's Docklands before it was redeveloped in the 1980s. Note the lack of open space. Land use maps show how the land is used – this shows the docks, housing and industrial areas. Roads, railways and services are not shown.

Map Key
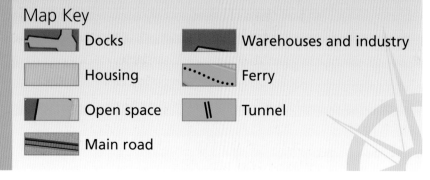

Docks	Warehouses and industry
Housing	Ferry
Open space	Tunnel
Main road	

SUSTAINABLE CITIES
Planners are now working to make settlements sustainable – to make sure they don't harm the environment as they grow. Recycling helps to reduce the amount of waste produced. Using less energy also helps the environment. Parks provide green spaces in cities. Waste ground can be made into parks. Reusing 'brownfield' sites for new developments helps to save wild areas.

LONDON DOCKLANDS

By the 1970s, London's Docklands had become run-down. Large ships no longer docked here, so the docks were disused. Local housing was run down and there was little public transport. In the 1980s, Docklands was rebuilt and transformed.

↑ **This photo of Docklands shows the new development around the tall tower of Canary Wharf. Disused warehouses are now modern apartments. There are also new offices, shopping centres, art galleries, roads, railways and a new airport.**

Look at the photo and the map

→ **The land use map doesn't show roads or railways, but it does show two forms of transport crossing the river. What are they?**

→ **Find Canary Wharf on the land use map. The curves of the river help to identify where this aerial view was taken. In what direction was the photographer facing?**

→ **Compare this land use map with other maps in the book. What differences can you see?**

TAKING IT FURTHER

• Find a modern map of London's Docklands in a UK atlas. Compare it with the land use map of the area before 1980. What differences can you see? How has transport been improved? What services are marked? Are there more open spaces?

• Use a library or local council website to find out about the changes planned in or near your settlement. How will the changes that are planned affect the environment? Try to find out what the council is doing to tackle the problems of waste and pollution.

Check your map skills

These two pages sum up all the map skills that have been introduced in this book. Understanding maps will help you to explore cities, towns and villages as well as the countryside.

WHAT ARE MAPS?

Maps are aerial views – drawings of the landscape from above. Maps use symbols – pictures, lines, letters or colours – to show features on the ground such as buildings, roads and rivers. The map key explains what the symbols mean.

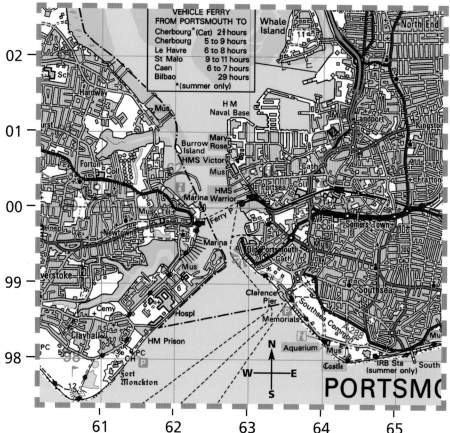

↑ The 1:50,000 map shows the centre of Portsmouth. Every 1 cm on the map represents 500 m (0.5 km) on the ground.

SCALE

Everything on a map is shrunk to a particular size. This is called drawing to scale. Small-scale maps such as 1:50,000 maps show a large area, but little detail. Large-scale maps such as 1:25,000 maps show a small area in more detail. The scale is marked on the map.

COMPASS POINTS

The points of the compass – north, south, east and west – can help you find your way. They can also describe the location of places in relation to somewhere else. On most maps north is at the top.

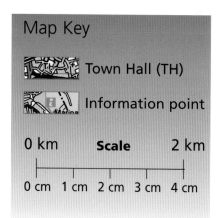

Map Key

Town Hall (TH)

Information point

| 0 km | Scale | 2 km |

0 cm 1 cm 2 cm 3 cm 4 cm

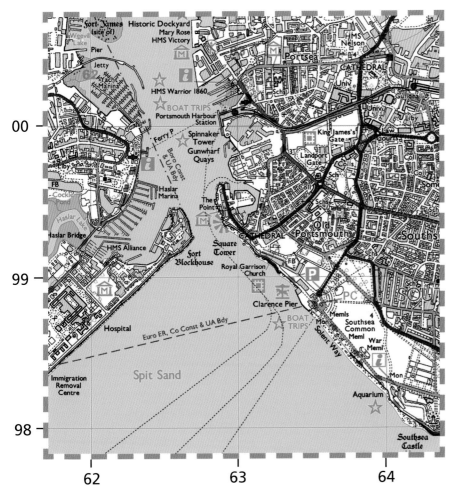

GRIDS AND GRID REFERENCES

The straight blue lines on maps form a grid of squares. Each side of the square represents 1 km. You can use this to estimate distance.

The numbers or letters on the grid allow you to pinpoint places on the map. The lines running upwards show east-west distances. The lines running across show north-south distances. Grid references give the east-west distance first, then the north-south distance. Remember "Along the corridor and up the stairs". The reference gives the bottom left-hand corner of the square.

↑ This 1:25,000 map shows Portsmouth Harbour in more detail. Every 1 cm on the map represents 250 m on the ground.

CONTOUR LINES

The ups and downs of the landscape are shown on the flat surface of maps using contour lines. These lines join places at the same height above sea level. On steep slopes contour lines are drawn close together. The heights of particular places are marked as numbers called spot heights.

0 km	Scale	1 km

0 cm   1 cm   2 cm   3 cm   4 cm

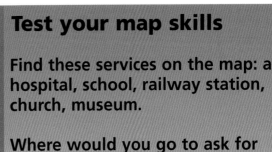

Test your map skills

→ Find these services on the map: a hospital, school, railway station, church, museum.

→ Where would you go to ask for information about Portsmouth?

→ How can you get across Portsmouth Harbour?

→ Where could you go to find out about sea life in square 6398?

→ Use the grid squares to estimate the distance between the Mary Rose and Clarence Pier.

Britain's towns and cities

This map shows some of Britain's largest towns and cities, plus all the places featured in this book. In the 1800s and 1900s, many of Britain's towns grew rapidly. Some grew so much that they merged with other towns in the area to form a settlement called a conurbation. These areas are shown in dark brown on the map.

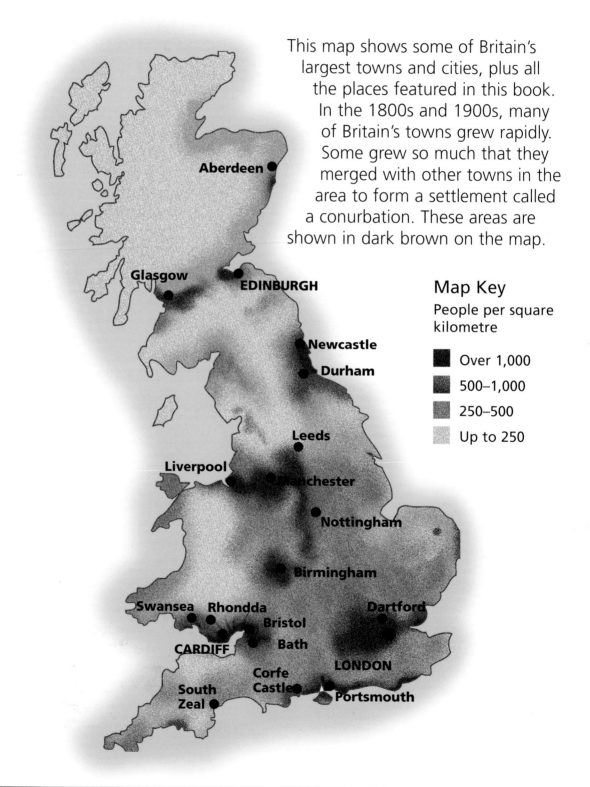

Map Key

People per square kilometre

■	Over 1,000
■	500–1,000
■	250–500
■	Up to 250

Aberdeen

Glasgow

EDINBURGH

Newcastle

Durham

Leeds

Liverpool

Manchester

Nottingham

Birmingham

Swansea   Rhondda   Dartford

Bristol

CARDIFF   Bath

Corfe Castle

LONDON

South Zeal   Portsmouth

Glossary

Aerial view A view of the landscape from above.

Brownfield site A place that has been built on that is not in use any more.

Bypass A road built to carry traffic around a settlement rather than through its centre.

City A settlement with about 100,000 people or more.

Commute When people from rural areas travel to a town or city to work.

Commuter belt The area around a city within which people commute.

Contour lines The lines on a map that show the height above sea level.

Conurbation A large urban area made up of several settlements that have grown and joined together.

Council The group of people or organisation that governs a settlement.

Ford A shallow crossing-point on a river, or to cross a river at a shallow point.

Found [a settlement] When the first buildings in a settlement are constructed.

Green belt An area around a city where building is carefully controlled.

Hamlet A small settlement that holds less than 50 people.

Industrial Revolution A period during the 1800s and early 1900s when many machines were invented, to do work such as weaving.

Industry A type of work. Industries include mining, manufacturing and tourism.

Linear settlement A long, thin settlement that grew up along the line of a road.

Location A place or the position of something.

Minerals The non-living substances from which rocks are made.

Nucleated settlement A round, compact settlement that grew up around a centre or nucleus.

Ore A rock containing a useful mineral, such as iron.

Ordnance Survey Britain's official map-making organisation.

Population The people who live in a particular place, such as a town or country.

Recycling When materials such as glass, plastic and tin are reused.

Residential Of or belonging to the residents of an area – the people who live there.

Resort A settlement to which people go for recreation or health reasons.

Rural Of or belonging to the countryside.

Scale The particular size a map is drawn to.

Settlement A place where people live, such as a village, town or city.

Services Features in a settlement that are available for people to use, such as a post box, public telephone, school or hospital, and also supplies of gas, electricity and water.

Sustainable Of a settlement, that does not damage the environment as it uses energy.

Symbol A sign or drawing that represents something else.

Urban Of or belonging to a town or city.

Index

FURTHER INFORMATION WEBSITES:

Websites about settlements:

For information on UK cities: www.dep.org.uk/cities
/CountryInfo/UK Info.htm

For information on new towns in Britain:
www.englishpartnerships.co.uk/newtowns.htm

Globaleye website has information about cities around
the world: www.globaleye.or.uk/secondary

Websites about maps:

Ordnance Survey: www.ordnancesurvey.co.uk/mapzone
www.multimap.co.uk Type in place names or postcodes
to see aerial views and maps of places in Britain

Websites about the environment:

Sustainable cities: www.sustainable-cities.org.uk/
Environment Agency: www.environment-agency.gov.uk
The National Trust: www.nationaltrust.org.uk/

Note to parents and teachers: Every effort has been made
by the Publishers to ensure that these websites are suitable
for children, that they are of the highest educational value,
and that they contain no inappropriate or offensive
material. However, because of the nature of the Internet, it
is impossible to guarantee that the contents of these sites
will not be altered. We strongly advise that Internet access
is supervised by a responsible adult.

These are the lists of contents for each title in *Mapping Britain's Landscapes:*